ESPIONAGE, INTELLIGENCE, RUSSIA, AND ME.

Spies, Lies, and Russian Misinformation.
BY BARRINGTON ROY SCHILLER

Spies, Lies, and Russian Misinformation.

Spies, Lies, and Russian Misinformation.

DEDICATION

I dedicate this book to all the unsung heroes whose names we will never know as their "track one point five" Diplomacy assignments, undertaken with plausible deniability for King, Queen and country, have been assigned to the annals of classified history.

Spies, Lies, and Russian Misinformation.

ACKNOWLEDGMENTS

All warfare is based on deception. Hence, when we can attack, we must seem unable; when using our forces, we must appear inactive; when we are near, we must make the enemy believe we are far away; when far away, we must make him feel we are near."
– Sun Tzu, The Art of War.

Spies, Lies, and Russian Misinformation.

CONTENTS

Spies, Lies, and Russian Misinformation.

Spies, Lies, and Russian Misinformation.

This document is told from the perspective of Me, Barrington Roy Schiller, and I offer it to the reader as a work of my experience in which some names have been changed. It is not comprehensive and may include misinformation and incorrect dates to allow "still classified" material to be included and protect living agents' identities.

However, the broad outlines are accurate, and I am a real person who was recruited by the West and did indeed travel to Cold War Berlin in 1971 to enter the world of Multinational NATO/SHAPE Cold War counterintelligence and Intelligence gathering: two closely related but distinct disciplines within the field of intelligence, and disciplines I have learnt since then. Despite being British, I was assigned to a Multinational unit and was housed in Roosevelt barracks. (closed in 1992) home of the 6941st Guard Battalion - a predominantly German unit assigned to provide security to US installations - and other miscellaneous units. My initial training involved learning covert investigation, interrogation and examination of NATO resources, security and facilities and counterintelligence inside buildings whose true purpose was disguised by signs misinforming their true purpose.

The book is based on extensive first-hand eyewitness research over 50 years, including my discussions with many of the people I knew in both NATO and Warsaw Pact countries during the Cold War. However, it is essential to remember that it is not an academic cited work, albeit based on extensive research, and so it should not be taken as a definitive account of my life, as I was once informed that were I to tell my "truth", my ability to renew my driving licence, passport or any other official document may be removed. As a result, I have taken some liberties with the truth to protect myself and others.

1

The role of military and soldier diplomats in the run-up World War II environment has been understudied due to a lack of data and knowledge of significant players for security reasons, and I hope that this creates a wedge to prise open the container that holds the stories of the many unsung heroes that gave their lives for King, Queen and country, that one day they receive the full recognition they deserve.

However, I hope it still provides an interesting account of pre-Cold War Germany's Intelligence landscape and as much information as possible about the major European Intelligence networks operating before that time. So as not to overstep the mark, I have only used freely available material and declassified to those who know what questions to ask and where to look, and perhaps as a signpost of where to look further for academics.

The book points at the complex relationships and motivations of the organisations involved, hopefully making it captivating for anyone interested in espionage and Cold War intelligence community history. Due to the confidential and covert nature of the work, there has been a lack of research on Intelligence and counterintelligence operations until now.

Although I do not doubt the loyalty and the integrity of British intelligence or any other organisations in the Intelligence community, working for "the greater good" is the name of the game. Hence, being "burnt" was an occupational risk. All assignments were given with plausible deniability to soldier diplomats, so all assignments were accepted on the premise that the only backup was a "possible" extraction" and should that not be possible, then all knowledge of the mission or connection to the "Intelligence gatherer" would be denied. Therefore, some views expressed here are those of the author and, for classified reasons, do not reflect the official policy or position of the Department of the Army, Department of Defense, or any government. The text includes a list of abbreviations and acronyms regularly used by defence and intelligence organisation professionals, and where possible, I have expanded upon them. This is the first of several books and mainly covers the period before the formation of the Soviet Union. I will pick up the chronology of the evolution of Intelligence in my next book.

Barrington Roy Schiller
Vigilia Pretium Libertatis

Before we look at the history of the ANGLO Russian intelligence and counterintelligence actors in this document, we must explore their terms of reference.

Abbreviations In this Book

AA (Soviet) Air Army

AAFCE Allied Air Forces Central Europe

ACGS(OR) Assistant Chief of the General Staff (Operational Requirements)

AI Air Interception (Radar)

ASTOR Airborne Stand-Off Radar

ATREL Air Transportable Reconnaissance Exploitation Laboratory

BAOR British Army of the Rhine

BFSU The British Forces Security Unit

BMH British Military Hospital

BSSO(G) British Services Security Organisation (Germany)

C2 Command and Control

DDR East Germany - Deutsche Democratic Republik

DIS Defence Intelligence Staff

ECM Electronic Counter Measures

EGAF East German Air Force

FCO Foreign and Commonwealth Office (Now FCDO)

FLM French Liaison Mission

GCHQ Government Communications Headquarters

GDR German Democratic Republic, i.e. DDR in German

GRU Glavnoje Razvedyvatelnoje Upravlenie - Red Army Intelligence Directorate

GSFG Group of Soviet Forces in Germany

IA Imagery Analyst

IR InfraRed

IRLS InfraRed LineScan

JARIC Joint Air Reconnaissance Intelligence Centre

JIC (G) Joint Intelligence Committee (Germany)

JSPI Joint School of Photographic Interpretation

KGB (Russian) Committee for State Security – Komitet gosudarstvennol bezopasnosti

LOROP Long Range Oblique Photography

MAREL Moveable Air Reconnaissance Exploitation Laboratory

SERB Soviet External Relations Bureau

MFPU Mobile Field Photographic Unit

MTI Moving Target Indicator

NBC Nuclear, Biological, Chemical

NOFORN 'No Foreign Eyes' - US national security classification

NVA Nationale Volksarmee. (the East German) National People's Army –

OP Observation Point

ORBAT Order of Battle – describes the identification, strength, command structure, and disposition of a military force's personnel, units, and equipment.

PRA Permanent Restricted Area

R&D Research and Development

RRF Radar Reconnaissance Flight

RSRE Royal Signals Research Establishment

SIS Secret Intelligence Service**ViPA** Vital Planning and Analysis uses Order of Battle (ORBAT) data to input into its calculations.

Vopo (East German) People's Police - Volkspolizei

SLAR Sideways Looking Airborne Radar

SOXMIS Soviet Exchange Mission

Spetznaz Soviet Special Forces – Spetsialnoje Naznachenie

Stasi (East German) State Security Service – Staatssicherheitsdienst

TASM Tactical Air-to-Surface Missile

TRA Temporary Restricted Area

USMLM United States Military Liaison Mission

1. EVOLUTION

This is the first book in my series of Books showing the evolution of East-West Military Intelligence, its advancements, Challenges, and the Need for International Collaboration in the Alphabet soup of Intelligence agencies when exploring the role of military intelligence, and it includes organisations up until the beginning of the Cold War.

The series analyses the advancements, challenges, and importance of International collaboration in this field and how Diplomacy and Military Intelligence often merge to create Track 1.5 Diplomats.

This work discusses the structures and authorities within the Russian and Western framework and how military intelligence evolved from being seen as an auxiliary function of warfare to a vital aspect of successful military operations. It highlights the shift from traditional intelligence sources to more direct methods of gathering information during World War I and the heavy reliance on intelligence during World War II.

This essay also mentions the emergence of open-source intelligence (OSINT) and the increasing use of tools like Artificial Intelligence (AI) in modern intelligence-gathering efforts.
It shows the roots of the challenges faced by NATO military intelligence gatherers in the face of new threats and the need for greater coordination amongst international partners in the form of strategies like drone surveillance, internet monitoring, and cyber-warfare.

Today, NATO's intelligence hunting plays a vital role in the national security and decision-making processes of over 32 Countries that still see a revanchist Russia as a threat. It recognises the significant technological advancements, methodologies, and the evolving nature of threats modern societies face. The essay highlights military intelligence's complex but necessary past and hopefully emphasises the importance of international collaboration to ensure maximum effectiveness against emerging adversaries.

2. WHAT IS INTELLIGENCE

First, we will look at the most common "types" of Intelligence and where they can be found.
It is said that the critical difference between intelligence and espionage is the collector's intent.

Intelligence or counterintelligence is usually considered a broader term for gathering information about governments or organisations, overtly or covertly, and it encompasses all means when collecting information to "protect national security". Espionage, however, is a more specific term that refers to the act of spying to obtain secret information, usually to "harm the national security" of another country by gaining a competitive advantage as if it were a zero-sum game.
Espionage is, therefore, typically conducted using a higher level of covert means, such as sneaking into a government facility to steal classified documents or recruiting others, such as spies, to do that.

Both may use deception or subterfuge to collect information, and they are often not mutually exclusive, and the "Missions" in post-WWII Germany indeed ran the gauntlet of both in their "Licensed to Spy" function. As quasi-diplomats, the Western Allies were permitted to "tour" and observe In Germany's Soviet-occupied zone, and they certainly pushed the boundaries by photographing and collecting military information while the Soviets attempted to keep it secret by trying desperately to protect and hide it from the prying Mission eyes closely. In a cat-and-mouse, sometimes lethal game, the Soviets and East Germans attempted to identify and track them to prevent them from stealing secrets and prevent it if they could.

In this book, I will generously describe the Mission's activities as "Intelligence gathering." and not as Spying while we focus on the evolution of Intelligence gathering and hunting from the Soviet Union and the Anglosphere.

Although, in many ways, the world has shrunk, and direct contact between people and information about them and their lives has become easier for anybody with a laptop, PC or smartphone to investigate, traditionally, we still reference the five main types of information gathering in the intelligence community nowadays as follows:-

HUMINT: Human intelligence involves gathering information from human sources, such as informants or spies, although, in modern times, the term "CHIS" (covert human intelligence source) is gaining popularity. With "West Germany" being far more wealthy than East Germany, the loyalty of East German informants could easily be tested by such simple items as Chocolate, leg warmers or whatever the latest trend was in the West, especially in those regions where they could receive Western TV. Then there were the West German travel spies who had relatives in East Germany, so they would visit East Germany with a list of wanted information so they could obtain it and report when back in the West. It could be as simple as the times of day Russian soldiers left their barracks to go to the local town or which bars they frequented. The "Stasi", East German state security and other Soviet countries had people"collecting, watching and reporting on their neighbours, and everything they saw.

IMINT: Imagery intelligence involves collecting information from images, such as aerial photography. Before satellites could read newspapers from their orbit, the transit paths from West Germany to Berlin and the Chipmunk kept at RAF Gatow resulted in some extremely creative flying to obtain irregular camera angles to extend the normal range of images available when flying horizontally. (Satellite photos were not freely available at the time).

SIGINT: Signals intelligence monitors electronic communications, such as phone calls or telegram messages. Etc

MASINT: Measurement and Signature Intelligence is an intelligence discipline built on measuring and capturing an object or activity's components and intrinsic characteristics. These characteristics allow the object or activity to be detected, identified, or characterised whenever encountered. In the case of Brixmis, this was as simple as placing a cigarette packet next to an item they were photographing to get a reference of the size.
And then, even before the Internet, there was **OSINT.**
Open-source intelligence involves collecting information that is publicly available from publicly available sources. Such sources as newspapers, news articles, magazines, posts in shop windows, and military documents were thrown away into bins, and any such information was of value to collect and take back to headquarters. Soviet soldiers in East Germany didn't have the luxury of toilet paper, so a friend of mine had the unenviable task of collecting the papers they used instead of toilet paper after they had finished their ablutions.
And then along came the World Wide Web with websites and social media. " Myspace!", a social networking service launched on August 1, 2003, was the first social network to reach a global audience and significantly influence technology, pop culture and music.

Zuckerberg launched "The Facebook" on February 4, 2004. to connect people around the university, but soon, it joined people worldwide.

In March 2006, Jack Dorsey, Noah Glass, Biz Stone, and Evan Williams created Twitter (now X).

Social media played a large part in the Arab Spring when people formed Networks online that were crucial in organising a core group of activists. Civil society leaders in Arab countries emphasised the role of the internet, mobile phones, and social media.

So before long, people were photographing and uploading everything they did to the "cloud" for Intelligence agencies and open-source expert journalists, like Bellingcat, to access. By gathering and analysing intelligence from a variety of sources, the intelligence community can help to identify and prevent threats, and it can also help to make informed risk analysis decisions about Domestic and foreign policy.

Nowadays, ignoring privacy concerns, people are fed the mantra of "if you have nothing to hide, then there is no reason to worry." CCTV is everywhere, and facial recognition tells us who they are. Covid allowed us to test how people would react if we locked them in their homes so Alexa, Siri, and a host of other "listening apps also spy on them.

However, nowadays, you don't need to be MI5 to practice open-source intelligence (OSINT) in this era of smartphones and social media. When a tank drives past a window outside its barracks, people can't help themselves. Each one has specific markings. They are not spies, but they take a picture and post it to the "socials" to show their friends. Then, Specialists like "Bellingcat " and Glavset, as well as citizen journalists, trawl, scrape and find every uploaded image of that tank and create a flip film of it as it moves towards its destination. This was most frequently used lately as Russia invaded Ukraine.

With AI, everybody can learn how to analyse photos and metadata, which, with "sock puppets", is becoming essential to avoid being fooled online.
The shadows tell us the sun's height, so the time of day, the leaves, the time of year, the garage next to the flats tell us the exact location with minimal research, etc.

Russia loves misinformation, but images lie unless you look at them as closely as the professionals. The same goes for facial recognition, finding people and their every movement. Even if alone, databases of backgrounds can identify exactly where and at what time of day the images were created.

The horrific example of ISIS beheading people was in the middle of nowhere, but analysts could determine the exact location and time by recognising the type of sand, weather, background scenery, shadows and even the most minor details. So even OSINT-MASINT can be used to track the movements of enemy forces, and IMINT can be used to identify their weapons and capabilities. MASINT can be used to determine the types of weapons being used, and OSINT can be used to track the activities of terrorist groups and other organisations.

The use of drones and other uncrewed aerial vehicles is expanding the capabilities of IMINT. And the development of new technologies, such as big data analytics and artificial intelligence, is making it possible to collect and process intelligence in new ways.

So, OSINT and other forms of intelligence gathering in the 2023 intelligence community are constantly evolving, and new types of intelligence are being developed, merging and being integrated all the time. So, even though Humint traditionally refers to humans gathering intelligence from other humans through direct contact, these five types of intelligence are often used to provide a comprehensive picture of a threat or situation.
Traditional Humint is when cells work with a handler identifying and recruiting "CHIS" (covert human information sources) to provide HUMINT. However, HUMINT can be used to identify and recruit those who can provide SIGINT or IMINT using OSINT. Still, the "CHIS" may no longer rely on interpersonal relationships, even if their specific talent is that of being a "honey trap". Honey trap operatives can be male or female, and in the intelligence community, foreign governments still use honey traps to gather

information from their rivals. They can also be used by private individuals or businesses to blackmail or extort their targets.

In George Orwell's "1984", people live in a world overseen by cameras and "Big Brother". That is the world we live in today, but what Orwell didn't predict was that not only would there be cameras on our streets, at our banks when we withdraw cash, and when we drive our car, but that GPS would track our every movement and that we would even pay to photograph and post our location, what we eat, and every detail of our lives online for "Big brother" to analyse, and Big Brother, has a name, "ECHELON".

"Echelon" is a global surveillance "counter-terrorism" program operated by the "intelligence community". The program is designed to collect and analyse communications data worldwide, including telephone calls, faxes, emails, and internet traffic. It is triggered by certain words, phrases and expressions that create alerts and with the "Internet of things", we tolerate that not only are you listening to your TV or radio, but they are listening to you, so you hear a joke and laugh, your friend laughs, Alexa, laughs, Cortana laughs, and Siri et al. laugh too. They all laugh. A friend once told me that they only listen when you say "Hello Alexa" until I pointed out that they must be able to listen all the time, or they wouldn't know when you say "Hello Alexa".

ECHELON is a highly secretive program whose existence was not officially acknowledged until the late 1990s. Even now, all the prompts and all the users are not made public. However, there is a lot of evidence to suggest that the program has been in operation for much longer than the Five Eyes network and that the intelligence gathered is available to Five Eyes, Nine Eyes, Fourteen Eyes, and others.

The exact capabilities of Echelon are unknown, but it is believed to be capable of collecting and analysing vast amounts of data, and this data can be used to track individuals, identify potential threats, and gather intelligence on foreign governments.

Echelon has been criticised for its secrecy and its potential for abuse. Critics argue that the program violates the privacy of individuals and that it can be used to target political dissidents and journalists.

The governments of Five Eyes New York have defended the echelon, arguing that it is a necessary tool for national security and that those who have done no wrong have nothing to fear. They also say that the program is subject to strict oversight and is not used to spy on citizens of the Five Eyes countries.

The program is a powerful tool that can be used for good or for evil, so it is essential to be aware of the potential impact of Echelon and to hold the governments of the five eyes accountable for its use when it:-

- collects data from various sources, including satellite communications, undersea cables, and fibre optic networks.

- analyses data in real-time and identifies patterns indicating threats.

- tracks individuals and groups across multiple communication channels.

- gathers intelligence on foreign governments and their activities.

Echelon is a powerful tool that can be used for good or evil.

It is essential to be aware of Echelon's potential impact and hold the governments of the five eyes accountable for its use.

So, imagine Echelon as the big brother of Alexa that uses specific keywords when people speak or write to create an alert every time it detects certain words that could be nefarious, and I assure you that there is no getting around it. Imagine artificial intelligence on steroids.

Criminals created "Encrochat", a Europe-based mobile phone communications network and service provider that offered modified smartphones allowing encrypted communication among themselves in the belief that they would not be caught, only to find that once the network had enough users, discussing their multiple organised crimes police in many countries swooped in and netted thousands of criminals who had been stupid enough to use the network to discuss their crimes. When it comes to criminal intelligence and especially national security, there is not and never will be one secure network on the planet.

The debate over Echelon will likely continue for many years to come, and the overarching question is how far we will accept the loss of our privacy to keep us "safe", especially now that governments worldwide have proven that they can mandate that we don't leave our homes so are subjected to house arrest (lockdown) when they order it, and we accept it.

3. THE INTELLIGENCE CYCLE

The intelligence community plays a vital role at all stages of our national security, and naturally, there are cases whereby intelligence (The product) simply lands in the gatherers' hands, but more often, it is a case whereby the community is constantly engaged in the continuous process of hunting for what they need to enter into the intelligence cycle. This ensures all interested parties have the intelligence they need to protect the alliances and members. The intelligence cycle usually consists of the following steps:-

Planning and direction: At this stage, the decision-makers (the consumers) define the required intelligence and in what order it will be collected. They then develop a plan and provide a forum for intelligence chiefs to discuss the intelligence requirements to support their operations and missions, choose a suitable intelligence collection agency (the gatherers) based upon the type of intelligence required, and direct them to collect the necessary intelligence (the product/s) for the operation.

Collection: Once the planners have defined what is needed, the collectors set out to collect the intelligence from various sources, including HUMINT (human intelligence), IMINT (imagery intelligence), SIGINT (signals intelligence), and MASINT (measurement and signature intelligence), according to the "collection plan". They usually do not plan the intelligence collection directly (leaving that to "planning and direction"), but they coordinate and oversee the collection activities. This ensures that all planners collect the necessary intelligence and that there is no duplication of effort.

Processing: Once collected the collectors do not process the intelligence directly. The collecting also involves converting the collected intelligence into a helpful format for analysis. The intelligence is processed to make it more beneficial to the consumers. This may include translating into different languages and transcribing or analysing intelligence data to produce insights and assessments. This ensures that all concerned comprehensively understand all the security threats.

Analysts examine and interpret the processed intelligence at the analysis stage to produce insights and assessments. This may involve identifying patterns and trends in intelligence or developing hypotheses about the intentions of adversaries. this ensures that all western allies use the same methods and tools to analyse intelligence and reach the same conclusions. analysts examine the processed intelligence to identify patterns, trends, and relationships. they also assess the reliability of the intelligence and its implications for their security.
dissemination: at the dissemination stage, the precise, concise, and relevant intelligence to the needs of the decision-makers is disseminated and communicated to the decision-makers and other relevant stakeholders and consumers in a timely and accurate manner. this ensures that decision-makers have the intelligence to make informed decisions.
feedback: this step involves collecting feedback from decision-making consumers on the usefulness of the intelligence provided and using that feedback to improve the intelligence cycle and find any changes that can be made to improve the effectiveness of the intelligence cycle. the allied decision-makers provide feedback to the intelligence community on the usefulness of the intelligence provided. a forum of intelligence chiefs discusses the feedback from decision-makers.

military intelligence has a long history, dating back to ancient civilisations, where espionage and reconnaissance were used to gain strategic advantages. however, the modern concept of military intelligence mainly began to take shape during the world wars. Studying intelligence history is a dynamic process, and new information is constantly coming to light. this is especially true in intelligence history, where formerly classified documentary materials change our understanding of how and why certain world events happened.

the above is naturally the "norm", but there are anomalies and exceptions. for example, the "missions" operated more like "scavengers" without knowing what they would find when they set out on their tours to gather. also, rather strangely, there were times when Brixmis (the British mission) would collect information and report it to the "allied pool" only to find that the US has then classified it as "noforn", which meant that no foreigners (i.e. those who had supplied the intelligence) were now allowed access to it. 9/11 proved how possessive different agencies were regarding "sharing". the alphabet soup of intelligence agencies hated sharing even with other agencies of their own country.

After the break up of the Soviet Union, the Russian Federation took the Honey trap one step further and sent an army of beautiful young women to marry men from "the West" and to have children with them, live for a while in "the West" before returning to their native Russia. You can take the women out of Russia, but you can't take Russia out of the girl. The dual nationality children are then Russified, and the Western fathers (who are nearly always influential) find themselves in a compromising situation, having to choose between their morals or their child.

4. SO NEAR, YET SO FAR

Just after dawn on 19th April 1775, the British attempted to disarm the Massachusetts militia. They failed, so on 4th July 1776, the Founding Fathers won the Revolutionary War and started a new country. They wrote the United States Declaration of Independence, signed the Constitution in 1787 and the Bill of Rights in 1791. General George Washington, who had led the war, became its first president. However, ever since those times, the UK and the USA have had a special relationship and have been the leading Allies of what came to be known as the "West".
Seldom have the two special Allies fought on the same side of any conflict or war as Russia, though. This juxtaposition has led many to believe that Russia and the USA were thousands of miles apart, ideologically and geographically.
The reality is that Russia and Alaska are only separated by the Bering Strait, and at its narrowest point, the Bering Strait measures only approximately 55 miles. Also, in the middle of the Strait, there are two Islands. The Islands are the Big Diomede, governed by the Russian Federation, and the Little Diomede Island, governed by the United States. The distance between the two Islands is just 3 miles (4.8 kilometres). These Islands shorten the geographical distance between Russia and Alaska even more.

Alaska once belonged to the Russian Empire, but they sold it to the USA, and Alaska was formally transferred to the United States on 18 October 1867 through a treaty ratified by the United States Senate.

However, rather than that being the end of the story, it was just
the beginning of centuries of rivalry between the two once-great
nations, with the British Empire watching from the sidelines in an
age when colonial empires clashed as they slowly but surely
shrank on the geopolitical stage with each vying to remain
significant and bathing is their past glories.

This is the story of what happened to those three countries but
not through the lens or level of analysis of the presidents, Kings,
Queens and rulers, but from the perspective of those behind the
scenes, providing the information for the rulers to base their
decisions upon and the lengths they went to, to prevent others
learning what their intentions were. This is the Machiavellian
world of those countries' backchannels, espionage, and
counterespionage.

5. FRENEMIES & THE RUSSKIY MIR: РУССКИЙ МИР

I am naturally not asserting that all Russians think the same or that all the Soviets did (after all, Stalin starved millions of Ukrainians to death in the Holodor, but not all Soviets did). I can't say that I have all the answers to the "Nature or Nurture" question in Russia either, but Foreign policy leads to the study of the "rational actor model", and to do that, a certain amount of knowledge regarding behavioural studies is essential in modern conflict resolution.

My first confrontation with the Russian World was in Berlin in 1972. The Cold War was raging, but the four Missions in Berlin had to work together. The Allied Control Council (ACC), represented by the Allied Kommandatura, played a vital role in the administration of Berlin during the Cold War. It was the four-power (American, British, Soviet, and French) body established by the Allies at the end of World War II to conduct the administration of Berlin, following an agreement at the Potsdam Conference of July-August 1945. It was responsible for all aspects of city government, including law and order, economic policy, and cultural affairs, so working with the Russian Mission "Soxmis" was essential, and even went as far as exchanging Christmas cards and gifts and attending social events together.

In Berlin in 1971, there was a complete Alphabet soup of agencies that symbolised the Four Powers' continued commitment to the city and its people, but the Kommandatura was also a forum for dialogue and cooperation between the four powers despite their ideological differences, and it was responsible for all aspects of the city's administration, including:

Maintaining public order and security

Providing electricity and essential services such as food and water

Overseeing the reconstruction of the city after the war
Enacting and enforcing laws and regulations
Conducting foreign relations on behalf of the city
The Kommandatura was also responsible for coordinating the activities of the four Allied sectors of the city. This task was challenging, as the four powers often had different agendas and priorities. However, the Kommandatura were generally able to agree on significant issues, such as the reconstruction of the city's infrastructure and the establishment a democratic government for Berlin.

The Allied Control Council (ACC) was multinational, and I lived in the US Roosevelt barracks despite being British.

People talk of the Russian-occupied zone (East Germany/ DDR/GDR) as a dark, glum place, but that was not the case for us. The average "Det A" pay in Berlin in 1971 was 450 Deutsche Marks per month. This was equivalent to about $225 at the time, but to maintain a sense of remaining incognito, my colleagues and I wore civilian clothes and were paid in Deutsche Marks. That being said, I'm sure that "they" knew who we were and "we" knew who "they" were, especially as the Imbiss Stube at the central train station (Bahnhof Zoo) was a common meeting place for the intelligence communities from both sides, whereas the Irish pub next to the ice rink at the Europa Center was more for meetings with handlers.

So, at the time, 1Dm = 8 Ost Mark or in the conversion rate of 21-year-old young men, 1 beer in the West was the same price as 8 beers in East Berlin, so it doesn't take much imagination to work out where we headed for after payday. Add to that the East German girls were also well aware that we were at least 8 times as wealthy as their East German workmates, and I'm sure that the allure of partying in East Germany becomes apparent, especially when one can put it down to HUMINT gathering. (I'm sure many of them felt the same, though) with them watching us, watching them. I always found the East Germans extraordinarily hospitable and was often invited back to their homes to meet parents who enjoyed speaking English.

Until the 4 + 2 agreement in 1991, which formally ended the Allied occupation of Germany (and to a lesser extent until 1994), nothing happened in the four occupied zones of Germany without the express permission of the Allied Control Council (ACC) much to the annoyance of the Germans.

If a head of State visited Berlin, they were greeted by a representative of the Kommantura first and only after that were they introduced to the Mayor to make the hierarchy clear and that the mayor was subordinate to the Allied Control Council (ACC), Allied occupation forces and the Kommandtura.

The 4+2 Agreement was a significant diplomatic achievement and perhaps cemented the birth of modern-day Diplomat Soldiers, Military diplomats, and their use of multinational military intelligence.

I remained in Allied Control Council (ACC) Occupied Germany, liaising with the Mayor's office and the chief Municipal Director's office of Braunschweig and Helmstedt (Checkpoint Alpha) and carrying out various assignments in Berlin, in the transit corridors, before marrying a woman first from West Germany, then from East Germany (Russian-occupied Zone), buying businesses in East Germany, marrying a Woman in Russia and having a son In Russia, and enjoying the company of many Russians while visiting Russian family. The Russians were always our adversaries and cordial but never enemies, with joint ACC Mission social events and Christmas cards being exchanged.

So, all in all, 50 years of engagement with Russians has enabled me to get an insight into Russia and its people, at home and abroad, although I will admit that my knowledge is based mainly on those from the European side of the Urals, and I know little of the Asian side, apart from relationships with several ladies from there.

The Russian world (Russian: Русский мир, romanised: Russkiy mir, lit. is complex and diverse. Tensions arising from regional identities and the government's efforts to balance unity with regional autonomy offer diplomats a nuanced understanding of Russia's internal dynamics and potential sources of stability or conflict.

Russia is a vast and diverse nation, encompassing various ethnicities, languages, and regions, and includes the works of some of Russia's greatest writers, such as Dostoevsky, Tolstoy, and Chekhov, as well as the films of Sergei Eisenstein, and Andrei Tarkovsky, which are considered to be among the greatest films ever made in the rich and diverse culture of Russia, and its love of ballet and opera.

'Russian world' ('Russian order', 'Russian community') is a concept and a political doctrine usually defined as the sphere of the cultural and political influence of Russia resulting from the Soviet legacy, which has had a profound impact on Russian society, but the Soviet Union left a legacy of corruption, inefficiency, and a lack of respect for the law, so it is now a thiefdom.

For the average Russian, nothing happens without a financial interest, which is certainly the experience I also have, as their very survival depends upon it. Suppose you don't have the finances to bribe officials. In that case, your life in Russia will be hell, or even non-existent, bringing about the rise of the oligarchs, an influential group of businessmen who have amassed great wealth through their connections to the government. Yet didn't Jane Austen want Elizabeth Bennet and her sisters to marry well, and have you ever tried to get a 2nd drink in an American bar if you didn't tip well after you got the first?

The "siloviki" (Strong men) have recently become increasingly prominent in Russian politics. Many siloviki, including President Vladimir Putin, have been appointed to high-ranking government positions. Siloviki are typically members of the Russian military, police, intelligence, or security forces. They are often seen as being very powerful and influential within Russian society. The term is translated as "people of force" or "strongmen" (from Russian сила, "force").

The "Russian world" concept primarily pertains to Russia's influence on countries with Slavic, Orthodox Christian, and Eurasian ties. This concept has gained prominence in Russia's foreign policy and relations with neighbouring states.

It has been a subject of significant discussion in geopolitics and International relations and is often associated with a shared linguistic, cultural, religious, political and historical heritage and the ties that bind them together.

It argues that this shared identity should be recognised and preserved to strengthen regional cooperation and influence on the global stage. As many countries have found, it is not easy to leave the influence of the Russian World.

However, the term "Russian world" is not without controversy, as its implications can vary depending on the context and the parties involved. Some view it as a way for Russia to exert its influence over neighbouring countries, potentially leading to concerns about encroachment on their sovereignty. This tension becomes particularly apparent in regions with significant Russian-speaking populations, where cultural and political autonomy debates can arise. For Russia, any country that has citizens who speak Russian Is Russian, and linguicide was commonly practised during the Soviet period to ensure that other languages were replaced by

Russian in schools so that the Kremlin-controlled their only source of information.

It's essential to consider the multifaceted nature of the concept. While some see it as a unifying force among certain nations, others view it as a tool for advancing Russia's political interests. As a diplomat and academic, you might find it valuable to explore these nuances further, examining both the historical basis and the contemporary implications of the "Russian world" concept in different geopolitical contexts and using different levels of analysis.

To summarise, the "Russian world" is a complex and debated concept with implications for geopolitics and national security. Its significance lies in its potential to shape Russia's interactions with neighbouring countries and its broader influence on the international stage.

In terms of suggested reading, one book that could offer valuable insights is "The 'Russian World': Russia's Soft Power and Geopolitical Imagination" by Marlène Laruelle. This work delves into the evolving notion of the "Russian world" and its role in Russia's foreign policy. It comprehensively analyses how this concept has been used and perceived domestically and internationally.

Between the collapse of the Soviet Union in 1991 and Vladimir Putin's ascent to power in Russia, several significant geopolitical and socio-political developments occurred that shaped the country's trajectory—this period witnessed profound changes in Russia's domestic politics, economic structure, foreign policy, and its standing in the international arena. Delving into critical events and factors influencing this transitional phase is necessary to provide a comprehensive overview.

Russia underwent a tumultuous political transformation following the disintegration of the Soviet Union. It was characterised by transitioning from a centrally planned economy to a market-oriented system, accompanied by political turbulence and economic challenges. The Yeltsin era (1991-1999) marked the beginning of multiparty politics in Russia, but it was marred by corruption, financial instability, and social discontent.

The post-Soviet period saw Russia grappling with the daunting task of transitioning from a state-controlled economy to a more liberal market-oriented system. This shift led to economic reforms, including privatising state-owned enterprises and establishing a new legal and regulatory framework for businesses. However, the rapid pace of reforms and inadequate institutional development contributed to the rise of oligarchs and a stark wealth disparity among the population.

The end of the Cold War led to a reconfiguration of geopolitical dynamics. Russia's status as a superpower was challenged, and the United States emerged as the dominant global player.

So, the period between the collapse of the Soviet Union and Vladimir Putin's rise to power was marked by complex domestic challenges, economic transformations, and a repositioning of Russia's role in the world. The transition from a superpower to a great power nation grappling with internal and external changes shaped the country's trajectory in the post-Cold War era. The rise of Putin shifted towards a more centralised and assertive state, with implications for Russia's domestic policies, foreign relations, and its position in the global order.

The Chechen conflict was one of the most notable domestic challenges. The First Chechen War (1994-1996) and the Second Chechen War (1999-2009) highlighted Russia's difficulties in controlling its diverse regions and addressing ethno-nationalist aspirations. These conflicts had significant implications for Russia's security policies.

Historical events, such as the Soviet era, on the collective mindset of the Russian people impact decision-making processes, political attitudes, and social cohesion. By understanding the collective perspective, diplomats can tailor their strategies to resonate with the values and aspirations of the Russian populace.

In 1999, Vladimir Putin, a former KGB officer, emerged as a key figure in Russian politics. He was appointed Prime Minister by President Boris Yeltsin and later succeeded Yeltsin as President in 2000.

Since 1999, Putin has held continuous positions as president or prime minister from 1999 to 2000 and from 2008 to 2012, he was prime minister, and he was president from 2000 to 2008 and has been since 2012.

Putin's leadership shifted the Russian Federation towards a more centralised and assertive state to restore Russia's influence and stability in the "Russkiy mir". As such, interactions with countries in the post-Soviet space, such as Ukraine, Belarus, and Moldova, about the "Russian world" have been particularly pronounced and intersect with broader themes like identity politics, nationalism, the creation of Frozen conflicts, and regional integration.

In a 2005 speech, Putin referred to the collapse of the Soviet Union as "the greatest geopolitical catastrophe of the century." These actions raised concerns among Russia's neighbours and pushed them into the arms of NATO, which strained its relations with Western powers.

Putin's presidency coincided with economic recovery driven by rising global energy prices. Russia's vast energy resources allowed it to influence international energy markets significantly. This newfound financial strength was leveraged to advance Russia's foreign policy objectives and strengthen its position on the global stage.

Putin is a strongman who has consolidated power and cracked down on dissent. The term "Responsibility to Protect" (R2P or RtoP) is a global political commitment endorsed by all member states of the United Nations at the 2005 World Summit to address its four key concerns to prevent genocide, war crimes, ethnic cleansing and crimes against humanity. Rather than "Responsibility to Protect", however, Russians under Putin have taken it as a "right to protect by any means they want", even if the protected country doesn't want their protection or puppet government.

Under Putin's leadership, Russia has pursued a more assertive foreign policy to reclaim its role as a significant global player. This was manifested in actions such as the conflict with Georgia in 2008 and the annexation of Crimea in 2014, as well as the total invasion of Ukraine in 2022.

However, I believe the Putin Regime's strategy is more of creating frozen conflicts by attacking and then bringing about a cease-fire, which only benefits Russia.

These conflicts are all located in the former Soviet Union and are characterized by the fact that they have not been resolved through a formal peace agreement. As a result, they remain a source of tension and instability in the region.

The Transnistria conflict is a conflict between Moldovan government forces and Transnistrian separatists. The conflict began in 1992, after the collapse of the Soviet Union. Transnistria is a strip of land along the eastern bank of the Dniester River, which is internationally recognized as part of Moldova. However, Transnistria has declared itself an independent republic, and it is supported by Russia.

The Nagorno-Karabakh conflict is a conflict between ethnic Armenians and ethnic Azerbaijanis over the disputed territory of Nagorno-Karabakh. The conflict began in 1988, during the last years of the Soviet Union. Nagorno-Karabakh is a mountainous region that is internationally recognized as part of Azerbaijan. However, the majority of the population of Nagorno-Karabakh is Armenian, and they have declared themselves an independent republic.

The South Ossetia conflict is a conflict between Georgian government forces and South Ossetian separatists. The conflict began in 1991, after the collapse of the Soviet Union. South Ossetia is an autonomous region within Georgia. However, South

Ossetia has declared itself an independent republic, and it is supported by Russia.

The Abkhazia conflict is a conflict between Georgian government forces and Abkhazian separatists. The conflict began in 1992, after the collapse of the Soviet Union. Abkhazia is an autonomous republic within Georgia. However, Abkhazia has declared itself an independent republic, and it is supported by Russia.

The Donbas conflict is a conflict between Ukrainian government forces and pro-Russian separatists. The conflict began in 2014 after the annexation of Crimea by Russia. The Donbas is a region in eastern Ukraine home to many ethnic Russians. The pro-Russian separatists have declared themselves independent republics supported by Russia.

These conflicts have had a devastating impact on the lives of the people who live in the affected regions. They have also contributed to the region's destabilisation and have made it more difficult to resolve other conflicts in the former Soviet Union.

As of November 2023, I believe Russia would consider their latest "Special Military Operation" a success if they can create a Frozen conflict reaching from Kharkiv to Kherson. This would enable them to negotiate the removal of certain sanctions and rest before completing their aim of connecting the frozen conflict dots. The majority of Russians genuinely believe that the previous Soviet territories BELONG to Russia and are occupied, waiting to be rescued from Western fascist Nazis.

Religious and cultural traditions are integral to Russian identity, and Putin has utilised the significance of Orthodox Christianity and its role in shaping Russian values and customs by using it for intertwining religious practices with national holidays and celebrations to support his "rebuilding" of the Soviet Union, providing insights into the cultural touchpoints that can facilitate mutual understanding and cooperation.

Russia has used oil as a weapon against other countries besides Ukraine. In 2014, Russia halted oil supplies to Poland, Lithuania, Latvia, and Estonia in what was seen as a politically motivated move.

Additionally, Russia has been accused of using oil as a weapon to force the countries into closer political and economic ties with Russia. It is worth noting that Russia's use of oil as a political tool has been a contentious issue in international relations, with some arguing that it is a legitimate exercise of power while others view it as an act of coercion.

Russia under Putin has also grappled with globalisation and technological advancement challenges, how these shifts impact traditional Russian values and behaviours, and dealing with generational dynamics and evolving attitudes toward innovation. Diplomats engaging with Russia can leverage these insights to foster collaboration aligning with historical legacies and future aspirations.

The Collective Mindset "Collectivism" has played a significant role in shaping Russian society. Together with Russian history, it has been marked by periods of adversity, resilience and historical events that have tested the Russian spirit, from wars to economic challenges. These experiences have shaped the national identity and fostered a sense of perseverance.

In economics and sociology, the "precariat" is a neologism for a social class formed by people suffering from precarity, a condition of existence without predictability or security, affecting material or psychological welfare. The term is a portmanteau obtained by merging precarious with the proletariat. Generally, Russians see themselves as downtrodden soulful artists, musicians and writers who have a right to patronage and the thanks of the whole world for them single-handedly defeating the Nazis, so the concept of reciprocity is non-existent. In the West, we expect you to buy me one if I buy you a beer. A Russian thinks, If he will buy me a beer, he will buy me dinner.

I have lived with several Russian women in several countries, and they are indeed cynical; you can take the girl out of Russia, but you can't take Russia out of the girl, so they see the whole world through a Russian lens of the Russian world, ignoring all geography, civil society, and any other facts. However, the stereotype that Russians are cold and inscrutable is far from accurate and is just apocryphal and stereotypical.

My 50 years of involvement with Russians at all levels include the one I married and had children with, dating several with contacts to all their friends and family, representing clients in courts, meetings in Embassies, bars, shops and generally out and about. I have always found them warm and friendly once you get to know them. Many can be extremely warm, charming and fun. However, I acknowledge that Russians can be challenging to understand, and their culture is often very different from Western cultures despite our joint appearance.

 A girlfriend, however, once explained to me that where she came from in Russia, only fools and idiots walked around smiling at strangers they didn't know and were just passing when I asked why she looked so solemn and scary. So, the Western "a smile is the shortest distance between two people" is not applicable when meeting Russians.

Here is a short story to demonstrate what I mean about all Russians expecting others to have been educated to have the same base values as they have.

An American student named John and a Russian student named Ivan were attending a demonstration. John and Ivan stood next to each other, holding signs and chanting slogans, and they got talking. Ivan asked John, "How much are you being paid to attend this demonstration?" John was surprised by the question and replied, "Nothing," he said. "I'm here because I believe in what we're fighting for." Ivan smiled and said "Yes, of course" but in such a manner that John realised that Ivan didn't believe him. It's true," John said. "I'm here because I want to make a difference." Ivan shook his head and laughed. "I don't believe you," he said. "Everyone who attends these demonstrations is paid to do so." "I know it's not easy," John said. "But we have to keep fighting. We can't give up." The government doesn't care about us. They're only interested in lining their own pockets." Then John asked Ivan, "Why don't you believe me?

Ivan answered, "I'm being paid to demonstrate here, so you must be too. Nobody would demonstrate without the permission of the government and being paid!

Russians, however, always think that others have the same base motives.

Effective communication is a cornerstone of diplomacy and international relations, and the nuances of Russian communication styles include indirect language, metaphors, and nonverbal cues. By dissecting common linguistic and behavioural patterns, we can decode underlying messages and bridge potential gaps in cross-cultural communication. There is, however, a typical Russian Communication style. Advanced students of the Russian language are often surprised to find that the same language that created such beautiful works is the most potent form of obscene profanity used in Russian and other Slavic language communities. "Mat" (Russian: мат, матерщи́на, ма́терный язы́к) is censored in the media, and "mat" in public constitutes a form of disorderly conduct punishable under Article 20.1. , but the concept of "mat" is deeply rooted in Russian culture and has a long history dating back to pre-revolutionary times. It is often associated with the working class and is seen as a way to express frustration and anger.

Some Russians also view the use of "MAT" as a way to demonstrate their toughness and resilience, so generally, westerners are usually quite surprised at how profane Russians often are. Some common examples of "mat" phrases in Russian include various curse words and vulgar expressions. These can range from mild to highly offensive, and their usage is generally inappropriate in most contexts.

While "mat" is not universally accepted in Russian society, it is still a standard part of everyday speech in specific contexts. It is essential to be aware of the cultural norms and expectations when using language in different settings.

Depending on the context, "mat" (vulgar and obscene language) in Russian culture is viewed differently by the audience. In informal settings, such as among friends or family, "mat" is often considered a normal part of everyday speech and is not seen as offensive. However, in more formal settings, such as in the workplace or public, the use of "mat" can be seen as inappropriate and unprofessional. Without understanding the nuance, don't use it, even if others around you do.

6. WHATABOUTISM

Should you engage with Russian trolls online or visitors and bring up the subjects of Human rights or Russian aggression, be prepared for a masterclass in public diplomacy from Russia and these Russian invasions to be dismissed with "Whataboutism" and "othering."

Remember, Russians have been fed the "Russian World" since birth, and that includes being the victims of Western hegemony, so they are ready for you. The Russian people are no different from others when it comes to being told negative things about their country, its leaders, or where they live. They don't like it!

The UK seems unique because it is almost a civic responsibility to criticise our politicians and civil society. It is so unique that we have dedicated a corner of one of Central London's parks as a speakers' corner for people to stand and openly criticise whatever they don't like.

Brits travelling abroad, however, should not try this in the USA as they will quickly tell you where to go back to if you criticise the

USA. And those living abroad should realise that much like my children, I can blame them, but don't you dare! The same goes for Russia.

Those in any corner of Russia standing on a soapbox and speaking, expecting just to be mocked as they criticise Russian policy on any matter, will soon find that speaking truth to power is not appreciated in the Russian Federation, so they will quickly find themselves imprisoned and taught a lesson in Russian "justice" in this one-party State where public political opposition is not appreciated or tolerated. As a result, any media freedoms are strictly State owned. So, if the State-owned media says, "All Ukrainians are Nazis, so we must invade to protect Russian speakers who are being oppressed, then that is what must be true", and all media and internet algorithms will feed them only the viewpoints that pander to that particular State confirmation bias.

One of the tools that the State does arm its population with, though, is " Whataboutism": a rhetorical defence that alleges hypocrisy from the accuser." (Khazan, 2013). If you speak to a Russian, you will rapidly learn that "whataboutism" and "othering" that are drilled into Russians in kindergarten and that International Relations students are like chess masters in using this Public Diplomacy technique.

Lecturers and professors you meet at conferences may not use it, but believe me; they humour you to be polite. They will be following the dominant discourse of their parents and just hiding either their shame if they think you are right or their anger if they have to listen to another arrogant Westerner spouting his imperialist views at them again so that they get what they want. Their media has engaged in "othering" for all their lifetime, and for the Russians, it is a definite case of them and "Us (the others)." Or, as they like to call us, "The West."

"Othering is perceiving or portraying someone or something as essentially alien or different. " 1865, James Hutchison Stirling

  It works as follows: You say "invasion of Crimea," they say, "What about Iraq? and the Serbians, who predominantly get their news from Russia, say, "What about Kosovo."
You say, "What about corrupt politicians in Russia?" and they contrast with, "What about crooked Hilary?" and an American president charged with multiple crimes, and so on.

You say police state; they say, "What about George Floyd and police brutality in the USA."

You say, "lack of Minority rights," and they respond with, "What about "Black lives matter."

You say RT is state-controlled, and they say the BBC is state-owned.

There is always a "whatabout" for any point you try to raise, occasionally leaving you to question your country's media presentation. After all, "what about the Native Americans protesting against the oil pipeline going to their ancient burial grounds? Why wasn't that more reported?

You may not follow Russian mainstream media, but you'll be surprised how well they follow yours.

The only problem is that the Russian Public diplomacy machine, with its warehouses full of trolls producing for "Kremlinwood" (and they say GCHQ), is too big and relies on the short memory of its audience as whataboutism can be contradictory, so relies on distraction rather than in-depth analysis.

Regarding Kosovo, Dmitry Medvedev says:-

1) " Kosova Independence violates Serbia's sovereignty and is a violation of international law" (*Dimitry Medvedev, Feb 2008*)

but then he contradicts himself when Medvedev wants to use Kosova to justify Russia's intervention in Sth Ossetia, Georgia, and he says: "In international relations, you can not have one rule for some (Kosovo) and another rule for others (Sth Ossetia) (*Medvedev, August 2008*)

There seems to be no problem even producing 2 "whatabouts" out of the same situation or even 3 when Medvedev is picked up on it and then claims that Sth Ossetia is a good type of Kosova. "Kosovo is a special case; South Ossetia is a special case " (Medvedev, August 2008). According to him, it is not appropriate to compare (whatabout) the two.
However, the one who really counts then uses Kosova again in a "whataboutism" to tell us that Crimea is just like Kosovo:" Crimea's secession from Ukraine was just like Kosova's secession from Serbia" "Vladimir Putin, March 2014).
Are you confused about Kosova? It provides an excellent example of "Whataboutism, " and confusion is precisely the aim. To 'whatabout" the West to recognise Kosovo is terrible, but it is good when Russia wants to justify the annexation of Crimea. So "Whataboutists" can't lose, and you won't care enough or be informed enough to argue further!
For foreigners, it is "If Kosovo is unique, then so is Crimea, so what about Kosovo? What is it that the Russians find so helpful about Kosovo? Those who have lived in both countries understand that Serbia sees itself as Russia's little brother, and for the Serbs, Kosovo is as much a part of Serbia ideologically and religiously as Wales is a part of the UK. Additionally, Russia has never bombed Belgrade, and most Serbian newspapers tow the Kremlin line; perhaps the EU should ask itself whether this cuckoo may be too big for their anti-populist agenda.

The men and women on the Serbian autobus are just as adept as the Russians at "Whataboutism" and disparaging views about the Imperial US who led NATO to bomb their beloved Belgrade and to leave cancer-causing depleted Uranium from the bombs NATO dropped.

"Whataboutism" has nothing to do with facts. It is more akin to mass conspiracy theory and comes from the birthplace of populism. It drives the listener to disregard their argument and tune in solely to the emotional part of the brain and, as such, is a highly valued state public diplomacy tool designed to get us to forget our rules and play by theirs.

Now, though, we don't need to go so far as Russia, Serbia or Kosovo. We have had our not-so-cold war called "Brexit," and "remainers" and "leavers" engage happily in polemic firing otherisms and whataboutisms at each other, with each side being armed by social media algorithms reinforcing and giving a positive bias to what they already believe with no hint of academic research or fact-checking.

Whataboutism and othering have seen significant growth in the UK since 48% of the British population who bothered to vote chose not to accept the decision of those who did and, like every punter buying a beer, know how to run the pub better and claim that they were missold as if the democratic election system was ever fair of perfect. It's not; it's just that the alternative is far less attractive for the typical person.

However, the good news for those who like speeding with no insurance or an expired driving license is that I was once with my father-in-law, and he was stopped by the police in Russia 3 times in one day, and $US20 each time solved the problem. Russian police are paid very little, so those speeding are seen as an excellent way to top up their salaries. The following week, he rolled his car in a 30mph (50 kmh) residential zone, yet he still continues to drive.

Ever since politicians realised that they could speak directly to populations of other nations and their own through social media and after the so-called Arab Spring called it "Public Diplomacy," the man on the street has believed that he now knows as much about diplomacy, and governance as do the qualified insiders who are involved daily in actually running and protecting the country. As a result, "illiberal democracies " have learnt how to block "unwanted" messages on their available internet URLs, so Russians only see what social media the State wants them to see despite proxy servers.

7. WELCOME TO ENTRY-LEVEL MASKIROVKA

In literal English, the Russian "maskirovka" is "a little masquerade" or a deception, and it comes as natural to Russians as drinking vodka.

It is complex, a cultural Russian phenomenon that is expected and of no surprise when others also use it. Russians expect to be tricked and misled, and so are proponents of "Trust but verify". Those in Intelligence gathering or law enforcement will recognise that as the English " Don't trust what you hear" or in some cases "what you see".

The Russian Federation Armed Forces have carried this military theory, doctrine, and thought forward since the intervening years between the collapse of the Soviet Union and Russia's newly found revanchism.

Maskirovka is part of Russian society culture and an essential aspect of Russian military operations. However, that is a game that two can play in military doctrine.

These tactics aimed at deceiving the enemy through camouflage, disinformation, and misdirection are an integral part of Russia's military strategy, with historical roots tracing back to the Soviet era. The concept of maskirovka encompasses a range of activities designed to obscure intentions, capabilities, and actions. This strategy involves a combination of both physical and information-based methods to create confusion and uncertainty among adversaries.

The Russian "Maskirovka," meaning "military deception," has a rich geopolitics and national security history. Its application has been observed in various forms over time. Below, I have compiled a small table that highlights some of the earliest examples of Russian Maskirovka:

If you talk to Russians, they will tell you that Ukraine is a part of Russia, so they have a right to reclaim it.

However, the Kyivan Rus, also spelt Kievan Rus, was founded by the Viking Varangian prince Rurik in 862, and the site of Kyiv had already been lived on for over 200 years by then, hundreds of years before Moscow.was founded in 1147. It also adopted Christianity as its official religion in 988. This period is marked by the rise of the Rus' state. The Rus was the Viking for "men with oars", and Rurik's successors were the ones that united the East Slavic tribes under their rule and created a powerful state that dominated Eastern Europe. The 11th-12th century is marked by the zenith of Kyivan's power and influence. Under the rule of princes such as Vladimir the Great and Yaroslav the Wise, Kyivan Rus became a major trade centre, culture, and religion nearly 300 years before Moscow was founded.

The Russian Federation would have you believe that they alone took Berlin in 1945, and although they are technically correct, they omit to explain that there are several reasons why the United States, the United Kingdom, and France (the Western Allies) waited for the Soviets for several days on the banks of the Elbe river and did not take Berlin in World War II.
At the Yalta Conference in February 1945, the Allied leaders had already agreed that Berlin would be located in the Soviet occupation zone after the war.

They had already decided to divide Germany into four occupation zones, and if the Western Allies had taken Berlin, they would have had to withdraw from the city again after the war. Eisenhower, however, decided to focus on encircling and defeating the German army in the Ruhr Valley. He also ordered his forces to advance to the Elbe River, which formed the boundary between the agreed American and Soviet occupation zones in Germany. The Western Allies reached the Elbe River in April 1945. They halted their advance there and waited for the Soviets to capture Berlin. The Soviets launched their final assault on Berlin on April 16, 1945, but didn't finish capturing the city until 8th May 1945.

The Western Allies also wanted to avoid the appearance of imperialism, and they had political concerns about taking Berlin. They did not want to be seen as competing with the Soviets for control of the city. The decision by the Western Allies not to take Berlin was controversial. Some historians have argued that the Western Allies should have captured Berlin. They say this would have prevented the Soviets from expanding their influence in Europe and sent a strong message to the Soviet Union about the Western Allies' commitment to democracy and freedom.
In Modern Russia, they ignore the four power agreements and

claim they won the "Great War" almost single-handedly while quoting and blaming America's late entry into the war for the number of Soviet losses, and they make a big deal of Germany's surrender to them.

What the Russians omit to say is that in Reims, France, on 7th May 1945, General Alfred Jodl, representing the German high command, signed an unconditional "act of military surrender" and that a cease-fire would go into effect at 11:01 p.m. Central European time on 8th May. This surrender was witnessed by General Ivan Susloparov of the Soviet Union, General Walter Bedell Smith of the United States, and General François Sevez of France. When soviet premier Joseph Stalin heard that Germany had signed an unconditional surrender of all its troops in Reims, he was furious. He argued that since the USSR had sacrificed the most troops and civilians during the war, its most important military commander should accept Germany's surrender rather than the soviet officer who had witnessed the signing in Reims. Stalin opposed the location of the signing, too: since Berlin had been the capital of the Third Reich, he argued, it should be the site of its surrender.
But Stalin's third objection—that Jodl was not Germany's most senior military official—would prove the most convincing to the rest of the Allies, all of whom remembered how the signing of the armistice that ended World War I had helped plant the seeds of the next world war.

Stalin argued that allowing Jodl to surrender to Germany in World War II could open the door to a new myth like the myths that had led to WW2 after WW1. Worried that Germany could again insist that its surrender was illegitimate if anyone but Field Marshal Wilhelm Keitel, the supreme commander of all German forces, personally signed the document, the Allies decided to restage the surrender.

 On 8th May 1945, Keitel headed to Karlshorst, a suburb of Berlin, to sign the document in front of Soviet Marshal Georgy Zhukov and a small Allied delegation.

However, Keitel had argued a minor point, hoping to add a clause giving his troops a grace period of at least 12 hours to ensure they received their cease-fire orders before facing any penalties for continuing to fight. Zhukov did not grant his request to add the clause but ultimately offered Keitel a verbal promise. This delay resulted in the document not being executed until after the cease-fire was supposed to begin—and the 9th of May had already arrived in Russia when Germany unconditionally surrendered again, and the second document was signed by Field Marshal Wilhelm Keitel, representing the German High Command, Marshal Georgy Zhukov of the Soviet Union, Air Chief Marshal Arthur Tedder of the United Kingdom, and General Carl Spaatz of the United States. General Jean de Lattre de Tassigny of France and General Dwight D. Eisenhower of the United States signed as witnesses. The second document confirmed and ratified the first one, and both declared the unconditional surrender of all German armed forces to the Allies.

For this reason, the Russians still celebrate the 9th May as victory day, and the Reims surrender wasn't even reported in the soviet press until a day afterwards, leading some observers to believe that the second surrender was a propaganda move orchestrated so Stalin could claim a more significant part of the credit for ending the war. In the rest of the world, though, v-e (victory in Europe) day is celebrated on 8th May, when the cease-fire was officially slated to begin.

It was introduced in 2005 as a new symbol of the Soviet victory in World War 2 by Putin's media. Since then, the ribbon has acquired many new horrible connotations. Among others, MH17 was shot down and plundered by people wearing this exact ribbon.

Another Example Of Russia's blatant "Bait and switch actions" (illegal advertising of goods, which are an apparent bargain, to substitute inferior or more expensive goods) is the Russian Federation's use of the terms "Russia" and the "Soviet Union". The Soviet Union was a "Superpower", whereas Russia (The Russian Federation) is, at best, "a Great Power".

Also, despite the Soviet Union no longer existing, the Russian Federation, as one of its components, has assumed the Soviet Union's position on the Security Council. Even though "if there is no Soviet Union, there can be no seat on the Security Council", and if any member of the Soviet Union is entitled to a place, then Ukraine is just as qualified as Russia.

Russia's favourite claim, and Bait and switch, however, is their claim that Russia lost over 20,000,000 in WW2. The following graphic, however, shows that as a percentage of the population, Russia didn't have the most significant loss in WW2.

So when the Russian Federation still claims that it lost more millions of its population than all others, it includes the population of many countries that it is now engaged in conflict with, and were there to be a war between West and East today, would fight AGAINST RUSSIA.

Even in Russia, there is minimal discussion about how many were from the Moscow/European side of the Urals and the less wealthy Asian side from where Russia's cannon fodder usually comes.

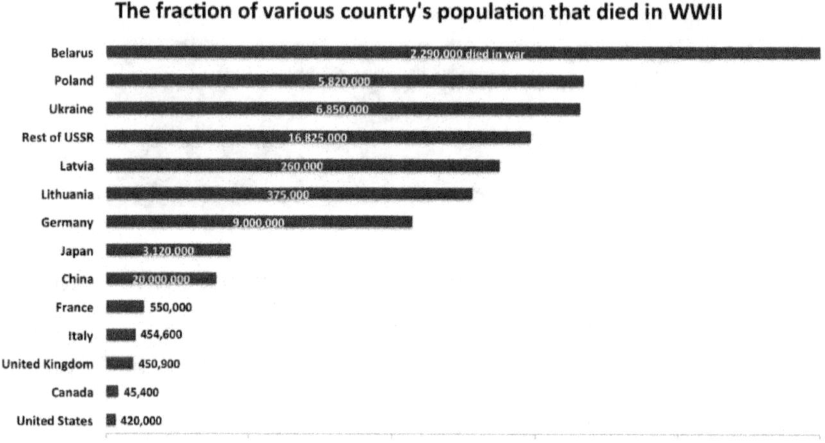

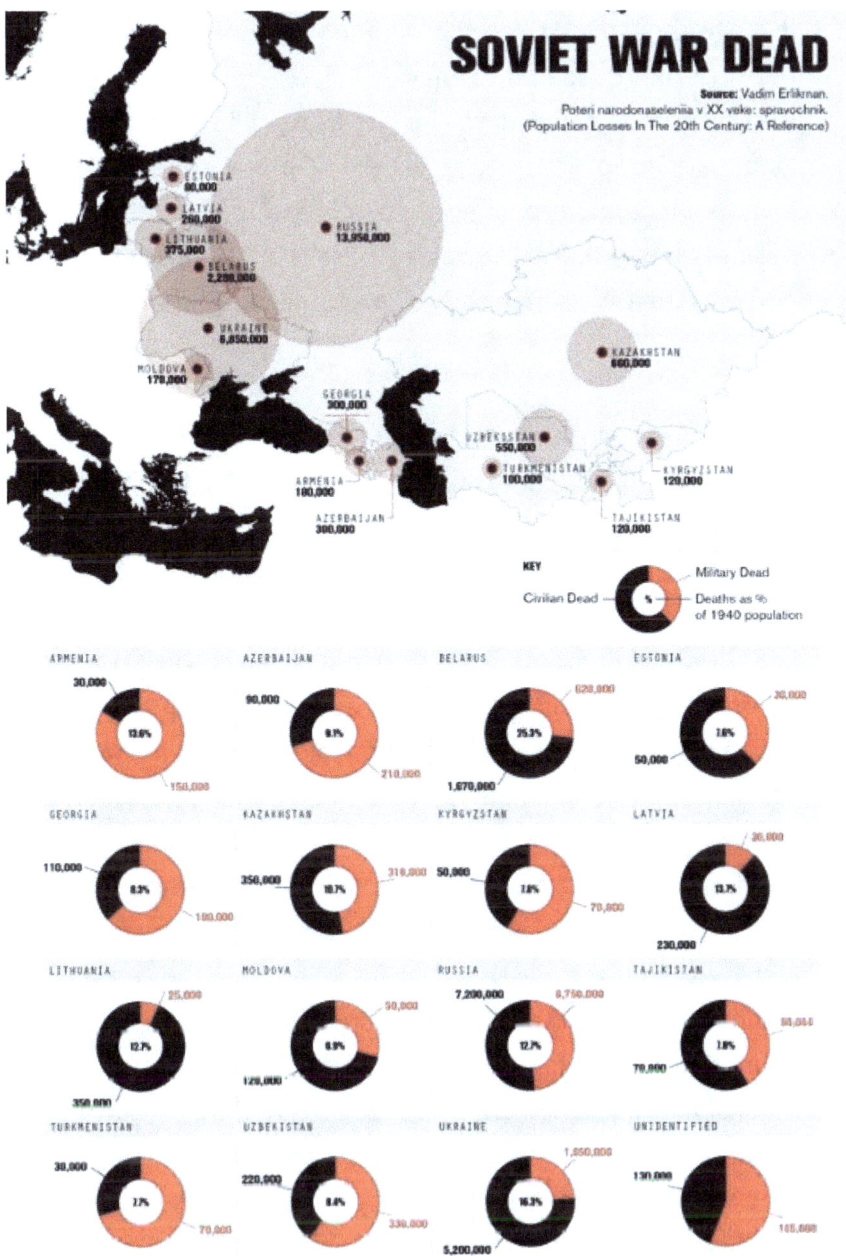

SOVIET WAR DEAD
Source: Vadim Erlikman.
Poteri narodonaseleniia v XX veke: spravochnik.
(Population Losses In The 20th Century: A Reference)
ESTONIA 80,000
LATVIA 260,000
LITHUANIA 375,000
BELARUS 2,290,000
UKRAINE 6,850,000
MOLDOVA 170,000
RUSSIA 13,950,000
KAZAKHSTAN 660,000
GEORGIA 300,000
UZBEKISTAN 550,000
TURKMENISTAN 100,000
KYRGYZSTAN 120,000
ARMENIA 180,000
AZERBAIJAN 300,000
TAJIKISTAN 120,000
KEY
Military Dead
Civilian Dead
Deaths as %
of 1940 population
ARMENIA
30,000
13.6%
150,000
AZERBAIJAN
90,000
9.1%
210,000
BELARUS
620,000
25.3%
1,670,000
ESTONIA
20,000
7.6%
50,000
GEORGIA
110,000
8.3%
190,000
KAZAKHSTAN
350,000
10.7%
310,000
KYRGYZSTAN
50,000
7.8%
70,000
LATVIA
20,000
13.7%
230,000
LITHUANIA
25,000
12.7%
350,000
MOLDOVA
50,000
6.9%
120,000
RUSSIA
7,200,000
6,750,000
12.7%
TAJIKISTAN
50,000
7.8%
70,000
TURKMENISTAN
30,000
7.7%
70,000
UZBEKISTAN
220,000
8.4%
330,000
UKRAINE
1,650,000
16.3%
5,200,000
UNIDENTIFIED
130,000
105,000

So, the Russians have taken this Maskirovka and turned it into a 21st-century Military precision art form.

In a warehouse in St Petersburg, Russia, "Glavset", also known as the "Internet Research Agency (IRA)", or the Troll factory, a Russian company linked to the late (is he?) Yevgeny Prigozhin of "Wagner Group" fame occupies the whole warehouse and engages in online propaganda to influence operations for Western business and political interests. There is an excellent film that portrays their work perfectly. "The Undeclared War" (TV Series 2022)

Glavset was founded in 2013 and has been accused of interfering in the 2016 United States presidential election, the 2017 French presidential election, and the 2018 Catalan independence referendum, amongst others. The company has also been accused of spreading disinformation about Brexit, the COVID-19 pandemic and the war in Ukraine, as well as the Hamas invasion of Israel. Glavset's operations are coordinated by a team of managers who assign tasks to teams of trolls. The trolls are paid to create fake social media accounts and post content that supports Russian interests or sow discord in other countries. They also use AI bots to amplify their messages and spread them widely. Governments and organisations around the world have condemned Glavset's activities. The United States has imposed sanctions on the company and its employees, and Facebook and Twitter have banned its accounts. However, Glavset continues to operate and is considered a significant threat to international security.

By targeting specific individuals or groups with their messages, they spread disinformation about political events or social issues, organise and support trade Unions and strikes, and try to influence elections or other public opinion. Glavset's activities are a severe threat to democracy and free speech.

Together with "Russia Today" RT, they undermine the ability of people to trust the information they see online and make it more difficult for them to participate in informed public debate. It is essential to be aware of Glavset's activities and to be critical of the information you see online, especially in these days of video and audio deep fakes spreading misinformation to pander to the confirmation bias of those who already doubt that their governments have their best interests.

Maskirovka is not new, though. These instances illustrate the historical use of Russian Maskirovka, encompassing diverse tactics such as misinformation, misdirection, and camouflage. They serve as intriguing case studies for exploring the complexity and effectiveness of such strategies in the context of geopolitical and military manoeuvring.

Year	Event	Description Source
1708	Battle of Lesnaya	During the Great Northern War, Russian forces created dummy camps to mislead Swedish forces, defeating them.
1812	Napoleonic Invasion of Russia	Russian forces used scorched earth tactics and false information to lure Napoleon's Grande Armée into a harsh winter, causing its downfall. Including camouflage, erroneous radio transmissions, and dummy divisions against Nazi Germany
1941	Operation Barbarossa	Soviet forces employed strategic deception,
1979-1989	Soviet Invasion of Afghanistan	Soviet forces utilised disinformation to downplay their involvement and intentions in Afghanistan, masking their true objectives.
2014	Annexation of Crimea	Russia employed a combination of military presence, misinformation, and deniability in its takeover of Crimea, creating confusion among observers.

Clifford, D. (2018). "Deception in War."

Zamoyski, A. (2005). "Moscow 1812."

Glantz, D. M. (2001). "Barbarossa Derailed."

Coll, S. (2005). "Ghost Wars."

Galeotti, M. (2014). "The Spetsnaz Threat."

Maskirovka has significantly shaped military operations and political manoeuvres in geopolitics and national security. It has been employed in various contexts, such as concealing troop movements, disguising the true nature of military exercises, and even manipulating public perception through disinformation campaigns.

One notable example of maskirovka was the Soviet Union's deception efforts during World War II. Operation Bagration, a massive Soviet offensive against German forces in 1944, was accompanied by an elaborate deception plan that included creating fictitious units, deceptive radio transmissions, and false orders. These measures aimed to divert German attention and resources away from the actual target of the offensive.

In the modern context, Russia's use of maskirovka has extended beyond the battlefield and into information warfare. The term is often associated with spreading disinformation and propaganda to manipulate public opinion and create confusion in the international arena. This approach has been evident in Russia's involvement in various global events, such as its annexation of Crimea in 2014 and its interventions in conflicts like the Syrian civil war.

To delve deeper into the subject, it's essential to explore specific historical instances and contemporary applications of maskirovka, drawing on academic sources and analyses. The works of renowned scholars in military strategy and international relations can provide valuable insights. For instance, John J. Mearsheimer's work on offensive realism ("The Tragedy of Great Power Politics") and Timothy Thomas's research on Russian information warfare ("Russia's 'New' Tools for Confronting the West: Continuity and Innovation in Moscow's Exercise of Power") offer comprehensive perspectives on this intricate topic.

In summary, maskirovka is a multifaceted concept deeply rooted in Russian military doctrine and strategy. Its historical significance and evolving manifestations in the contemporary geopolitical landscape make it a compelling subject of study and discussion for diplomats, scholars, and practitioners in geopolitics and national security.

8 INTELLIGENCE ROOTS

The concept of intelligence gathering was not new for the four Allied powers when WW2 was thrust upon the world, as any mediaeval scholar will testify. I am not a historian, so I will leave the in-depth research to those who specialise in those periods of history and will focus solely on signposting to those organisations that serious scholars may wish to focus upon in depth while I give brief descriptions in a semi-chronological order and only focus on the four WW2 Allied powers for my fellow lay persons to consume.

After establishing the basic principles of what textbook Intelligence is, how we deal with it, and then examining our most frequent adversary and sometimes ally in the 20th century, it would be remiss of me not to look at the last hundred years of who the major players have been.

I will begin this chronology in the 19th Century, and although I am not a historian, nor do I speak Russian, I have attempted to lay out the information relatively chronologically. Serious scholars should, however, use the data as indicators for further study and not as 100% accurate.

The "British Secret Service " was England's first modern intelligence agency. It was founded in 1800 by William Wickham, the Home Secretary, and like modern-day MI6, it was mainly formed, responsible for foreign intelligence, to gather intelligence on the activities of foreign governments and organisations. i.e. Napoleon Bonaparte and the French Empire. It was responsible for gathering human intelligence, or HUMINT, and conducting covert operations. It was renamed *MI6* in 1909. However, in 1916, the bureau was split into two organisations: *MI5*, responsible for domestic assets and security, and MI6, responsible for foreign intelligence. It is a misconception that deals with all matters in the UK and MI6 all matters abroad. MI5 (Security Service) protects British assets, including Embassies abroad, from threats such as terrorism, espionage, and sabotage. MI6 (Secret Intelligence Service) is responsible for collecting intelligence abroad and does not have a direct role in protecting British assets.

In Russia, *The Prussian Military Intelligence* (1806-1918) was founded in **1806** in response to the defeat of Prussia by Napoleon Bonaparte at the Battle of Jena-Auerstedt. It was responsible for gathering military intelligence on the activities of Prussia's enemies. It was disbanded after World War I.

In 1810, a precursor to modern Russian military intelligence agencies was established under Tsar Alexander I of Russia, named *Chancellery of Foreign Corps - Канцелярия иностранных корпусов* which was also known as *the* **Foreign Corps Office**(1810 to 1825). It operated during the early 19th century.

The Chancellery's primary focus was gathering and analysing intelligence about foreign nations' military activities, capabilities, and international political developments. This included monitoring the activities of developments that could impact Russia's military interests, and the Chancellery of Foreign Corps contributed valuable intelligence to Russian military command during various conflicts. It aided decision-making by providing insights into the intentions and movements of foreign military forces. The Chancellery employed military officers, diplomats, and analysts to conduct intelligence-gathering activities. These individuals gathered information from various sources, including open sources, diplomatic channels, and informants for the Russian command during multiple conflicts.

It was part of a broader effort to improve the Russian military's intelligence-gathering capabilities.

While the Chancellery of Foreign Corps was not a long-lasting institution, it enhanced Russia's military intelligence capabilities during a crucial period in European history. It laid the groundwork for subsequent developments in Russian military intelligence, establishing more formal intelligence agencies in the following years. The reasons for its dissolution are unclear, but it could have been due to changing priorities or shifts in intelligence-gathering methods.

The Decembrist Revolt (**26 December 1825**) was a failed attempt to overthrow the Russian monarchy, and it resulted in Tsar Nicholas I appointing a member of the Imperial Cabinet"who was also chief of gendarmes" to form a secret police agency and intelligence agency in the Imperial Russian Empire to monitor and suppress political dissent, investigate revolutionary activities, and maintain surveillance over potential threats to the Tsarist regime. **This Russian Ministry of the *Interior branch was The Third Section of the Imperial Chancellery, also known as the Third Department.* (1825 – 1880)** The primary functions of the Third Section included conducting surveillance, intercepting mail, monitoring political and intellectual circles, monitoring the activities of foreigners in Russia, enforcing censorship, and gathering intelligence on individuals and groups deemed suspicious by the government. Its activities extended to both domestic and foreign affairs. It was also responsible for the Tsar's security and played a significant role in maintaining the monarchy's power amidst growing concerns about political unrest and revolutionary movements within the Russian Empire. The Third Section was essential in suppressing various uprisings, such as the Decembrist Revolt and the Polish Uprisings of the 19th century. It was responsible for identifying and apprehending individuals involved in these movements. The Third Section was also responsible for the imprisonment and execution of thousands of people as a significant force in Russian politics for over 50 years. The Third Section used various methods to intimidate and silence its opponents. It employed a network of over 1,000 informants, spies, and agents to gather information and censors responsible for censoring all printed material, including books, newspapers, and pamphlets. It often used coercion and intimidation to extract information and suppress dissent. Its activities were characterised by secrecy and a lack of transparency, and it had its own prisons and interrogation chambers. The Third Section's activities were characterised by a repressive and often brutal approach to maintaining order and quelling dissent. It represented a time of intense government surveillance and control over political actions, and it reflected the autocratic nature of the Russian Empire during the 19th century. The American Pinkerton National Detective Agency (1850-1983) was founded in 1850 by Allan Pinkerton in the USA. The Pinkerton Agency was not an official intelligence agency, but it did provide intelligence services to the United States government. The Pinkerton Agency gathered both HUMINT and SIGINT or signals intelligence. It ceased operating in 1983, but its name and logo were acquired by Securitas AB in 1983, a security company not affiliated with the original Pinkerton Agency. We can, therefore, claim that it was but is no longer in operation.

***The French Deuxième Bureau** was founded* **in 1871** in response to the Franco-Prussian War. The Deuxième Bureau was responsible for gathering military intelligence on the activities of France's enemies. It was disbanded after the fall of France in World War II. In 1880, Tsar Alexander II abolished the Third Section as part of his efforts to implement reforms in the wake of the assassination attempt on his life.

The Third Section in Russia was replaced by a more moderate political police organisation called *the **Department of Police of the Ministry of the Interior**,* but the Third Section's methods of repression and surveillance were later adopted by the Soviet secret police (the KGB). Its legacy reminds us of the dangers of unchecked power and the importance of protecting civil liberties. However, its legacy also continued to haunt the Russian Empire and lives on

In 1881the Okhrana was officially established by Tsar Alexander III following the assassination of his father, Tsar Alexander II. So, from the late 19th century until the Russian Revolution of 1917, the Okhrana, officially known as "the Department for Protecting Public Security and Order under the Ministry of Internal Affairs of the Russian Empire", was the secret police and intelligence agency of Imperial Russia.

Concerns about the rise of revolutionary and terrorist movements had prompted the agency's creation, and the Okhrana's primary objective was to maintain the security of the autocratic regime, suppress political dissent, and monitor revolutionary activities. It also undertook counterintelligence to identify and combat foreign espionage and disrupt foreign intelligence operations and political policing in Russia to suppress domestic opposition. It monitored revolutionary organisations, intercepted mail, conducted surveillance, and infiltrated radical groups like those before the Okhrana, and it employed a network of agents, informants, and spies to gather information. It often used covert tactics, provocations, and deception to identify and neutralise revolutionary elements. One of the most prominent Okhrana agents was Yevno Azef, who infiltrated and manipulated revolutionary groups. His actions raised suspicions and accusations of double-agent activities. The Okhrana was involved in repressive actions against various revolutionary movements, including socialist and nationalist groups.

It played a role in suppressing political dissent and revolutionary activity, the 1905 Revolution and efforts to promote political reforms. The Okhrana's activities and methods contributed to growing discontent and opposition to the Tsarist regime.

The Office of Naval Intelligence (ONI) *was Founded in* **(1882-ongoing)** as the United States Navy's intelligence organisation. As of 2023, it still provides intelligence support to naval operations, including information about naval forces, maritime security, and geopolitical developments that could impact U.S. naval interests.

"Special Branch" is the British police unit responsible for counter-terrorism and security intelligence. It was formed in 1883 to investigate Fenian terrorism in the UK after the surge of rural violence in Ireland in the 1870s, which peaked during the Land War of 1879–82 and was regularly referred to as Fenian terrorism. On 22nd August 1883, Fenian 'Red' Jim McDermott was arrested.

On 31 August 1883, Those responsible for the Glasgow bombings in January were arrested.

On 30 Oct 1883, Two bombs exploded in the London Underground, at Paddington (Praed Street) station (injuring 70 people) and Westminster Bridge station.

On Various dates from 1909 and during World War I, **the British War Office** established various "MI" (Military Intelligence sections) to handle specific intelligence tasks.

MI 1 focused on geographical intelligence,

MI 2 on codebreaking,

MI 3 on censorship,

MI 4 on propaganda,

MI 5 (as part of the Directorate of Military Operations) on domestic counterespionage terrorism and security to protect the UK and its assets from espionage and subversion. It is responsible for protecting national security by countering espionage and other threats. MI5 gathers intelligence on any individuals and groups deemed a risk to national security.

MI 6 on foreign intelligence. MI6 is responsible for foreign intelligence and espionage operations. Its focus is on gathering information from foreign governments, organisations, and individuals to support British national security and foreign policy goals,

And MI 7 on propaganda distribution.

The (British) Intelligence Department, which initially collected information on foreign military forces, geopolitical developments, and potential threats to British interests, was established within the British War Office to address intelligence needs in preparation for World War I and was dissolved just before the breakout of WW1 in 1914. Today, we know its descendent as the Secret Intelligence Service (SIS)

The Military Information Division was established in 1886, collecting information on U.S. and foreign armies. It Acquired responsibility for supervising army military attaches on April 19th, 1889, and on March 18, 1892, its responsibilities were expanded to include issuing military maps and other informational publications and acting as a liaison between the Office of the Secretary of War and state militias.

The Military Information Division was established in 1886, collecting information on U.S. and foreign armies. It Acquired responsibility for supervising army military attaches on April 19th, 1889, and on March 18th, 1892, its responsibilities were expanded to include issuing military maps and other informational publications and acting as a liaison between the Office of the Secretary of War and state militias.

WDGS Second Division was designated on August 15th, 1903, responsible for collecting, arranging, and publishing military information, including that on foreign armies, administering the army military attache system, maintaining the War Department Library, preparing war maps, and preparing campaign histories.

The second Section was abolished, with functions of the Military Information Committee to the newly established War College Division, where they were vested in the Committee on Military Information, which also continued to be known as the Military Information Committee and was designated the Military Information Section for appropriation purposes.

On April 28th, 1917, it was redesignated "Military Intelligence Section", confirmed on May 3rd, 1917, and then further redesignated "Military Intelligence Branch" and assigned to the newly established "Executive Division" on February 9th, 1918. The "Executive Division" was abolished, and the "Military Intelligence Branch" was redesignated "Military Intelligence Division" on August 26th, 1918. Records of the War Department General and Special Staffs [WDGS/WDSS] can be found here for those who wish to study further: https://www.archives.gov/research/guide-fed-records/groups/165.html#165.4

9 THE COLD WAR

As we have shown, the Intelligence community took root in East-West bloc relations long before WW1 and has never left the continent of Europe despite significant changes in the global security environment.

It is important to note that the Cold War was not a traditional war. The Cold War was fought on many fronts, including the political, economic, and technological spheres. It was a time of great uncertainty and fear as the world lived under the threat of nuclear war. There were no significant military conflicts between the United States and the Soviet Union, but there was a long period of tension and rivalry between the two superpowers. Some argue that it was the most prolonged period in Europe without War.

There is no official definition of who first coined the expression "Cold War", but there are various people to whom it is attributed. Some say the term "Cold War" was first used by George Orwell in an article published in 1945. Orwell understood it as a nuclear stalemate between "super-states.", which brought about MAD (Mutually assured Destruction). The United States and the Soviet Union competed to develop more and more powerful nuclear weapons, and this arms race led to great tension and fear between the two countries, but each possessed weapons of mass destruction and could annihilate the other, so they didn't use them but continued the arms race and started using proxies to fight their battles.

Others attribute it to Bernard Baruch, an American financier and presidential advisor, in a speech in 1947.

However, I take Winston Churchill's March 5, 1946 "Iron Curtain" speech, warning of the Soviet threat to Europe, as my start date of the Cold War.

Here is an excerpt from Churchill's Iron Curtain speech:

"From Stettin in the Baltic to Trieste in the Adriatic, an iron curtain has descended across the Continent. Behind that line lie all the capitals of the ancient states of Central and Eastern Europe. Warsaw, Berlin, Prague, Vienna, Budapest, Belgrade, Bucharest and Sofia, all these famous cities and the populations around them lie in what I must call the Soviet sphere, and all are subject in one form or another, not only to Soviet influence but to a very high and, in some cases, an increasing measure of control from Moscow."

Whoever coined the term is irrelevant, as espionage became the focus of their activities as the United States and the Soviet Union competed to be the first country to send a person into space, and this space race further increased the tensions between the two nations.

The USA was only one of the Allies, and the Soviet Union wasn't a country but a group of countries, so it would be more accurate to describe this as a conflict between "Washington and its supporters" and "Moscow and its supporters" in which both avoid direct conflict since they realise that they exist in a "MAD" environment, with both understanding that a hot war would be Mutually assured Destruction because both sides have enough Atomic warheads to destroy each other multiple times should they be used.

Although no single date marks the start of the Cold War, some historians argue that it began with the 1917 October Revolution in Russia, when the Bolshevik Red Army overthrew the *Russian Provisional Government.*, the white army. The Bolsheviks supported the Russian Red Army, led by Vladimir Lenin. The

Bolsheviks were a communist party that wanted to overthrow the Russian monarchy and establish a socialist state. They were also supported by the peasantry, who were attracted to the Bolsheviks' promises of land reform.

The Russian White Army was supported by the Whites, a coalition of different political groups that opposed the Bolsheviks. The Russian aristocracy, the military, and the wealthy supported the Whites. They also received support from foreign powers like France, Britain, and the United States. This is certainly a date that Russians consider to be the start of their "disagreements with "THE WEST." as is the date when the Soviet Union formed after the Russian Civil War, which ended in 1920 with the victory of the Bolsheviks. The Bolsheviks, led by Vladimir Lenin, wanted to create a socialist state in Russia. They believed the Soviet Union would be a model for other countries against the wishes of "The West".

However, some historians argue that it began in 1945 when the United States and the Soviet Union disagreed about the postwar order in Europe.

Russia also conveniently forgets the Molotov–Ribbentrop Pact and prefers only to remember when they fought the Nazis as Allies of the West. At the beginning of WW2, the Soviet Union and the Nazis signed a non-aggression pact on 23rd August 1939. The treaty also included a secret protocol that divided Eastern Europe into spheres of influence. The Soviet Union agreed to allow Germany to annex parts of Poland, Finland, and the Baltic States. Germany permitted the Soviet Union to annex Bessarabia and Northern Bukovina from Romania. The Molotov–Ribbentrop Pact was a significant turning point in World War II. It allowed Germany to focus its military on the West, while the Soviet Union was able to consolidate its power in Eastern Europe. The pact also led to the outbreak of war between Germany and Poland, which began World War II. So they were Allies of the NAZIs until the Nazis turned upon them in 1941 and became allies of the West, allowing them a victory which they have dined out on with great pomposity every year since.

They like to claim all 20 million Soviet deaths as Russian deaths without considering that just under 50% of those deaths were military from other Soviet Union countries, most of whom are now more aligned with the Western allies than with Russia and are even physically at war with Russia in the case of Ukraine. Indeed, one of the most significant events that contributed to the start of the Cold War was the breakdown of the Yalta Conference of February 1945. At this conference, the leaders of the United States, the Soviet Union, and Great Britain agreed on the post-war division of Germany. However, the agreement soon broke down as the Soviet Union began to consolidate its control over Eastern Europe while the United States and its allies worked to rebuild Western Europe.

The tiny Communist parties, which were in all these Eastern States of Europe, had been raised to pre-eminence and power far beyond their numbers and were seeking everywhere to obtain totalitarian control."

Police governments prevailed in nearly every case, except in Czechoslovakia, and there was no true democracy in any of them." "In many of these States, life for the individual citizen had become difficult. Many newspapers and periodicals had been suppressed or were strictly censored. There was no freedom of speech, no freedom of information. Churches were being emptied, and the Catholic Church, in particular, was under severe restrictions. There was a widespread sense of discontent and unrest." "The Soviet Government had shown itself unwilling to allow free elections in any of these States. It had shown itself unwilling to permit the establishment of independent trade

unions. It had shown itself reluctant to allow the formation of independent political parties. It had established itself determined to maintain absolute control over the life of these States.
" Churchill's Iron Curtain speech was powerful and influential. It helped shape the course of the Cold War and remains relevant today. The speech is a reminder of how dangerous totalitarianism is and the importance of freedom and democracy.

However, if Churchill's Iron Curtain speech lit the fuse, President Harry Truman announced the Truman Doctrine In 1947, which pledged US economic and military aid to any country resisting communist aggression. This was in response to the Soviet Union's attempt to install a communist government in Greece.

United States President Harry S. Truman delivered the Truman Doctrine speech on 12 March 1947 before a joint session of Congress.

In his speech, Truman outlined a new policy of American foreign aid to help countries resist communist subversion. Truman declared that the United States would provide economic and military assistance to any nation fighting communist subversion. The Truman Doctrine directly responded to the situation in Greece and Turkey, where communist-backed rebels were fighting against the government. Truman argued that the United States had a moral obligation to help Greece and Turkey resist communism and that if they fell to communism, it would threaten the entire Middle East. He announced that the United States would provide economic and military aid to Greece and Turkey to help them resist communist subversion.

Truman's speech was met with widespread support in the United States. Congress approved $400 million to aid Greece and Turkey, and the Truman Doctrine became the foundation of American foreign policy for the next four decades and was a significant turning point in the Cold War. It marked the beginning of the

United States' policy of containment, which aimed to prevent the spread of communism.

As a response to the growing threat of communism in Europe, the speech also helped to solidify the United States' role as the leader of the Western Alliance. The Soviet Union had recently installed communist governments in Poland, Hungary, and Romania. Truman feared that the Soviet Union would continue to expand its influence in Europe, and he wanted to clarify that the United States would not stand idly by.

The Truman Doctrine is considered one of the most important speeches in American history, and the critical points of the Truman Doctrine speech declare that:

The United States will support free peoples who are resisting attempted subjugation by armed minorities or by outside pressures.

The United States will not disregard aggression and subversion in other parts of the world.

The United States will provide economic and military assistance to any country resisting communism.

The United States will not allow any country to fall under the domination of a totalitarian power.

The United States will help free people to work out their destinies in their own way.

The United States will provide economic and financial aid to countries struggling to resist communism.

The United States will work with other countries to promote peace and democracy.

The Truman Doctrine speech was a controversial turning point in the Cold War. It was met with mixed reactions. Some people praised Truman for his commitment to fighting communism and said it was necessary to contain the spread of communism, while others criticised him for being too interventionist, which led to the Cold War.

The Truman Alliance was not the only factor that contributed to the division of Europe into two spheres of influence. Most historians argue that the Cold War was, however, certainly solidified in 1948 when the Soviet Union blockaded the western part of Berlin. The Berlin Blockade occurred in 1948 when the Soviet Union blocked all land access to the western part of Berlin under Allied control. The Allies responded by airlifting supplies to the city, and the blockade was eventually lifted. These events began intense rivalry and tension between the United States and the Soviet Union. However, the Hungarian Revolution (1956) also played a role in the Cold War.

The two countries were now clearly on opposite sides of a global ideological struggle, and the Cold War had begun.

However, even during times of dangerous tensions in the East-West/ Washington -Moscow confrontation, backchannels and non-Track one diplomatic channels had to be retained so Brixmis and the other military Missions remained essential to prevent a cold war from becoming a hot war at a time of fear and suspicion, which had a profound impact on the world.

It was a time, however, which also led to some positive developments, such as the development of new technologies and the growth of international cooperation, despite the number of regional conflicts in Europe since the end of WW2, a cold war and Mutually assured Destruction between Washington/ NATO and Moscow/GRU has resulted in no new war since 1945, giving us the most extended period of peace in Europe forever.

International relations look at Wars as typically more severe than conflicts as they are often seen as a threat to international peace and security, and states are more likely to intervene in wars than in conflicts.

10 EPILOGUE

The frequency and intensity of traditional state-on-state war has declined since 1945. This shift is attributed to factors such as establishing the United Nations and the proliferation of international institutions to prevent and resolve conflicts peacefully. Additionally, the nuclear arms race created a deterrence against large-scale conventional wars.

While state-on-state wars have decreased, intrastate conflicts, also known as civil wars, have become more prevalent. These conflicts are typically fought between different groups or factions within a single country, often over identity, political power, or resource control issues.

However, non-state actors, such as rebel groups, militias, and terrorist organizations, have played an increasingly prominent role in modern warfare, as have proxy wars. These actors often employ unconventional tactics, such as guerrilla warfare and asymmetric warfare, to challenge state authorities and pursue their objectives.

As a result, it is not so much that the original Intelligence cycle has been replaced, but now, much like the space race, an Intelligence technology race is underway. At all stages of the Intelligence Cycle, technology and artificial Intelligence assist the Human face of our endeavours, and technology costs vast sums of finance, so although non-state actors often have access to large amounts of finance, the Deep State and its deep pockets define the odds of the Machiavellian Intelligence world in 2023.

ABOUT THE AUTHOR

From Berlin in 1971 to Ukraine in 2024, the Author, Barrington Roy Schiller, has been active in all aspects of the Intelligence Cycle throughout Europe and all NATO and Warsaw Pact Countries. From gathering to planning and directing, he has extensive knowledge of how Intelligence works in both the overt and the covert environment. In 2023, while writing this book, he was active as a Private diplomatic Track 1.5 Contractor.

www.ingramcontent.com/pod-product-compliance
Lightning Source LLC
Chambersburg PA
CBHW060756260726
48660CB00002B/654